Wild Homes

Written by Rob Alcraft

Collins

What makes a home?

Wild homes are made with lots of skill!
They help keep their owners safe.

Let's take a look.

Dig holes

Rabbits go underground to stay safe.

They dig a warren of holes and burrows in the earth.

Groups of rabbits share a warren.

Make a mound

Termites make tall, steep mounds of earth.

The mound helps their nest stay cool.
A typical mound takes years to make.

Chew!

Wasps chew dead trees into a pulp.
They make their smooth, round nest from
the pulp.

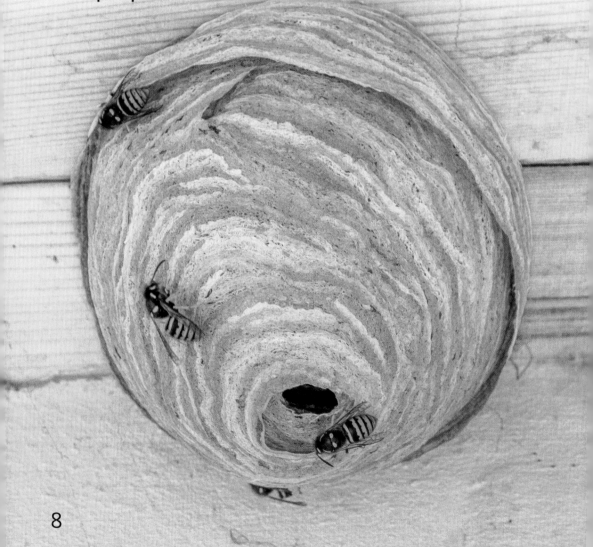

The queen lays her eggs inside the nest.

Thread grass

Weaver birds thread nests among tree branches.

If a nest shows skill, the bird could attract a mate.

Borrow a home

Hermit crabs don't grow their own new shells.
They borrow an old shell as a home.

Inside it is safe.

Cut down trees

Beavers cut down trees to slow down a river's flow.

Pointed teeth cut the trunks.

Beavers make a home with branches in the still pool.

Make a web

A cobweb is part home, part trap.
Insect prey collides with the threads
and becomes caught.

The spider waits – then strikes!

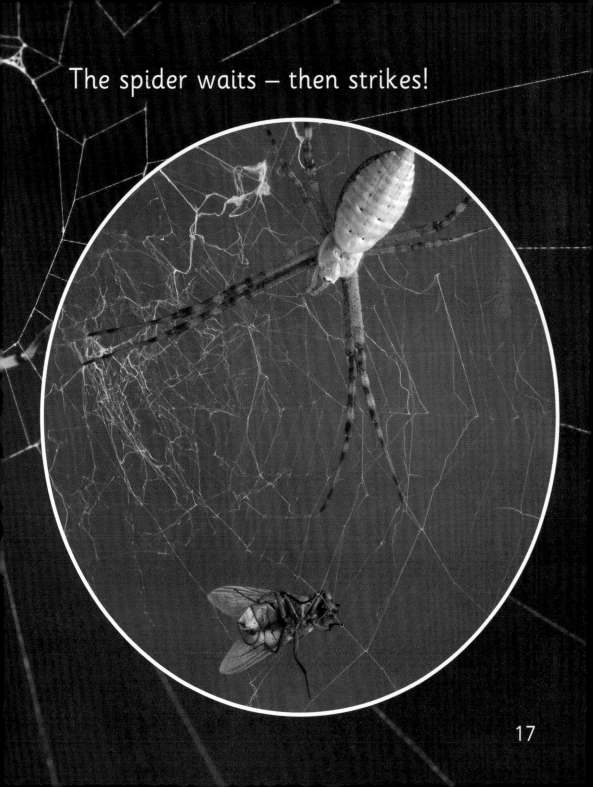

Show off!

Bower birds make their homes to impress a mate.

They seek out items that suit their home.
This bird likes blue!

Home, sweet home!

Each wild home suits its owner. Some help the owner to stay safe, some trap food and others are for showing off!

21

What home?

keeping safe

staying cool

trapping food

showing off

23

After reading

Letters and Sounds: Phase 5

Word count: 249

Focus phonemes: /igh/ i, i-e /ai/ ay, ey, a-e /oa/ o, ow, o-e /oo/ ue, ew, ui, ou /ee/ ea /ow/ ou /oo/ oul /ar/ a /or/ augh, al /air/ are /ur/ ir, ear /e/ ea /i/ y /o/ a /u/ o

Common exception words: of, the, to, into, are, what, their

Curriculum links: Science: Animals, including humans

National Curriculum learning objectives: Reading/word reading: read accurately by blending sounds in unfamiliar words containing GPCs that have been taught; Reading/comprehension: understand both the books they can already read accurately and fluently and those they listen to by checking that the text makes sense to them as they read, and correcting inaccurate reading

Developing fluency

- Your child may enjoy hearing you read the book.
- Talk about how we can read non-fiction with expression to make it interesting for the listener. You could read a page aloud as though you are narrating for a wildlife programme. Ask your child to do the same.

Phonic practice

- Ask your child to sound talk and blend each of the following words:

  s/m/oo/th   ch/ew   b/l/ue   s/ui/t   g/r/ou/p

- Ask your child:
  - Can you tell me which sound is the same in each word? (/oo/)
  - Can you point to the letter or group of letters that represent the /oo/ sound in each word? (*oo, ew, ue, ui, ou*)
  - Can you think of other words that contain the /oo/ sound? (e.g. *zoo, flute*)

Extending vocabulary

- Look at page 7. Ask your child if they can think of another word that could be used instead of **mound**. (e.g. *hill*)
- Look at page 8. Ask your child if they can think of another word that could be used instead of **smooth**. (e.g. *even, flat*)
- Look at page 17. Ask your child if they can think of another word that could be used instead of **strikes**. (e.g. *attacks*)